FIRE FOR THOUGHT

FIRE FOR THOUGHT

REED BYE

BLAZEVOX[BOOKS]
Buffalo, New York

Printed in the United States of America

Interior design and typesetting by Geoffrey Gatza
Cover art: "Latest Reality" by Bobbie Louise Hawkins, collection of
Anne Waldman. Printed with artist's permission. Photo by Ann Klein.

First Edition
ISBN: 978-1-60964-234-1
Library of Congress Control Number: 2015954033

BlazeVOX [books]
131 Euclid Ave
Kenmore, NY 14217

Editor@blazevox.org

publisher of weird little books

BlazeVOX [books]

blazevox.org

21 20 19 18 17 16 15 14 13 12 01 02 03 04 05 06 07 08 09 10

BlazeVOX

Table Of Contents

Acknowledgments

Several of these poems have appeared in the following magazines and journals: *Denver Quarterly*, *Fact-Simile*, *Summer Stock*, *Embodied Poetics*, and *Bombay Gin*.

FIRE FOR THOUGHT

for Jill

with great love and appreciation

HOW IT BEGINS, WITH STEPS

into the unknown. A thin skin
leads us on, one who can see the way
a fox does and has felt the wind
collapse his home. What is left?
A length of wire and when that runs out
a tender dream stands above
breasts bared, smiling

The sun was sharp
Bits and pieces shared its course
What was then discovered? The job one has
to do. It lit the way
that flowed in currents, adjusting
balance side to side

How does one get rid of the lumps
with heart of previous day intact
or with a new one starting? Breath
reads symptoms, makes its diagnosis
and prescribes what truth to take
Flag flaps, spoon stirs. Lift and
swallow

GO TO IT, EVERY DETAIL

of the surface, pond and cattail
mountain, sky, and limb
Just below their feelings for each other
what can I do—Hearts of geese incline
and land on water, a sure sign
we have this power growing through our fingers
that into others in the scene enroots
a system inter-animating logic

Water guides our footprints
Lip and tongue talk down that avenue
that leads to what's becoming sorcerous

Come, everything that seems to be implores
to bed, and feel a kindred flame
These kinds that grow together in the night
   A mind like bindweed
   forms a saddle
rides on turtles, landing in the evening
    woven into time-threads
    thinking and forgetting
what it is to rise and bob and duck and go

ONE CAN HARDLY SIT STRAIGHT ENOUGH

The shell already cracked
Who knows what's breeding in that core
A new generation
Who knows how time will warp genes
            this time
running up and raising lumps
            hauled by trucks
through basements and
across the cornfield
taking down phonelines with
a copy of Ode to the West Wind
            in one hand
and something from Leaves of Grass
stuffed in the other pocket

            Be careful
about that bulb in your projector
and the newspaper shifting its beam
whose point of view, already late
for the next frame
is a tiger pacing. A millisecond
            later
it bounds into the present
Last scene: Fred and Ethel
standing at the door in wide-eyed wonder

WHAT IS IN THE WIND

Coming from so many directions at once
to frighten and set the stage for
        more discomfited angels
        spreading feathered seeds
A toss-up—dirty work
testing strength of stem, armed to
        depth of root in clay
Is it narrow with a purpose?

What is to be protected from such
        fleeting motivation
and what is its relation to inevitability
        and power?

We supplicate the wisdom of space
Chokyi Gyatso. What will become of the lore
        this ore
if adharmic forces win
this breeze, so fresh and sharp
        and what it seeds

FIRE FOR THOUGHT

for Anne and Ambrose

Pleased and re-pleased shocked and dragged
life finds itself bumping against the V of a fork
misunderstanding, swirling
into a side channel, popping out
with deeper currents folding underneath
Something opens and closes
Occasional pieces form a puzzle
Questions swirl habits
breeding more delusion ecstasy and
disappointment—Going along
in my twenties and then life comes up big
with marriage and a child, lives on either side
nudging   Altered momentum
Happy accidents   Meeting the dharma
Living persons   Primordial wisdom
Life and its problems   Sit on the bottom
Get with the breathing
Enter the world   bigger than thought
Native condition   bigger than I thought
Feeling the value   Insight of non-thought
Part of the current   Mind that can know
How is it possible   Knowing itself
beyond what can know it   Consort of learning
Unending tether   Out from the flame
Into the ether   Into the stream

HOW'S THE FLAME?

You know what you have taken in today
looking at an eight-legged specimen
standing and playing harp in a group
        Punctuation as
        point of entry

Sailing off into the branch
        of a neuron
inescapably, teeth
        rattle at the intersection

Brain encased by a skull
        with holes
        larger than theaters

Bus after bus
        full of the guilty
Now there you go
Fire the editor! Cool morning flagstone
        magenta lichen
        adjusting one's socks
Get it together—rein in thinking
Put the bigger cauldron back on simmer

GREETINGS

everyone associated with the pure present
A salutation!
So full and alive in the arteries
Whatever you do next will
climb continental shelves
to get back home
      Come
           indigo moon
lean out from your divan and lend
a floating light to each one
being washed up on the shore

As flares explore artifacts
raked from grasses, cast your glance
    on tide pools
Blame and remorse stand delivered
    in waves overlapping—
These clans and countries you have known

COMING TO A BOIL

A veil, smokeproof
hanging in the midst
Is that a problem?
Yes, according to the soothsayer

No, opposed the poet
Think of it as brave
milk
where "Heidigger" comes from, lots of leaves

caught in his hair
so-going, finding its way
through
warp and woof. How else—

sun appearing to be gone
stay eclipsed?
The rest aglow—dappled leaves
exchanged for patience

Giving names a
desolation, through whose veil
things disperse—
lids flapping up and down

SAY IT WAS ALL UNDERSTOOD

There was this church and it was
crow child squawk for
fresh fallen snow
A congregation
lapsed by limbs that
knew the stairs but couldn't find the
sanctuary

When empty tracts once neighborhoods
that now no longer do what things
one did who had the grace but lost the drift
of what was said that used to
catch the light and
set aglow its rays

The world time forgot's
remembered on a thread
The colors that produce a tear become
a palette quaking
Nothing that was said before—
Who's holding this vast puppetry
aloft?—provides a handle

Don't you want to get it going?
Cock on a walk, gray day
Sun stuck in its lock

SO MUCH IMPULSE NOW ENCLOSES

Earth jelly
Sorrow but no concern
Too much inside, nothing out
            risen with the sun
See the battered leaves of squash
evening-influenced, dressed in sincerity
spilling forth. Things respond
                        with simple
            elegance
                        angling
                            into orgasm
Only a little
style moves into confusion—
Can't understand them
Aren't humans much? There is no limit
            to what they think and
                        try to understand

Appearance at one edge
            squashed
                        and joy, the
            open-hearted renovator, at the other
                        an angled jackhammer
                        bringing it all back up

SAME DAY

Pushing and turning this way and that
like brushes in a generator
memory cannibals feed
while mothers pour others cups of tea

All the blazing retinue—
sharks in riot gear with penny whistles—
arc the canyon, making waves
No one to point out the inconsistency

Correspondence in immediacy
crazed for one moment
tripping on barbed wire, falling in dung
One aching thought after another

Nothing to gain
Not even drama
No thrill-a-minute hours and days
Old memory, first discount store

Wide aisles, empty shelves
Outside, rainclouds
The sweatband of my father
driving, stopped at a railroad crossing

This poem appeared on the back of a truck
in a green band of light and dust

MY OWN HEART CERTAINLY SANK

Now only a beam protrudes
"I'm going to ask him to do something"
she says pointing at me, and won't say more
but chops distinctly at the air—
How characteristic I think, annoyingly

My so-called self largely composed of
hair and memory loss. C'est la vie
mothers and sons, mothers alone, every
child not so free of links
recorded as a braid of lights
You barely emerge you're so weighted down with
drapes and other object-symbols

Quizzical looks, a dying fall
as you see and know the world
one way or another you are mother of
        You crowned
or otherwise emerged with own head
and now must move a pollywoggish form
through bigger waters to a town

A street with others stratified in time
Come along and do the calamari
Stroke the humpback with a budded twig
Trail and propel yourself at once
It's all about the angles body takes
planing forward on a heart that beats
its way across an oceanic globe

MIND AND BODY

O are you dead, poor thing, that just had life
here in the midst of the miraculous
frame that spawns motion and confusion
and like a song that's gone, comes back
as fainting inspiration

Upon a stream in which a tiny bark
uplifts and keeps its series
tacking back and forth in time like
skateboards in a park, a panoply
No one has too much to gain

Sorting fibers in a third-floor warehouse
A mouse above on violincello
Note for note a life like yours
in different runs the wind combs through
grain-headed grasses on a plain

Lark-sparrow on a fence
As times go we don't see you anymore
We don't know to what degree you dined
on seeds and berries while you lived
This mention made here, elsewhere none

cared for long—
The world lived in you and now you're gone
The world lives again and now you're back
a little creaky in the knees perhaps
but less afraid within the shade of rushes

CUTTING BOARD

Powerful monkeys
bombard the intermission
with bliss capsules
as a trapdoor of family news
opens cautiously to let me in
concerned about my being so temporary

A love of art?
What kind of thought is that
they ask. Rich and spontaneous
here as probe
remembering just what things
have and how much time's remaining

Food, musical instruments
a 350 lb. Siberian tiger
Delights of existence we cannot
hang onto, offered as continuity of
that which comes without
remorse

Jewel facets, crocus light
It hardly matters
Extended hand
I offer
in hopeless emulation
Everyone who tries will be forgiven

SUCCESSION

A long time schoolgirls waited
for the bus and boys ran
toward a shoe store
stopping on a dime with one foot planted

A door slams life goes on
less sure. Was it planned that way?
Stitched and stretched
and snap the girls wake older

Not old enough the boys
could not guide thread through
needles bent and then the sky rained
Life will make its leaps of force

When closing down in sex was not so tender
as juicy meat was once and not so now
Trust holds the lid
Wind reaching in and pushing up

the heels of lightweights. Boys
and girls lean against each other
travelling paths of ancestors
just enough tread still on their tires

THIS AND THAT MET

They didn't have nerves yet
but angled sideways toward each other
One did its best but wasn't much
Wore a scarf and looked away
Arrived in town on a rain delay
Stones falling from the sky
and one girl on a platform
under a dripping eave

Many years pass the other comes closer
without a thought
but adamant. This lasted due
to angles that were good
for balance on the planks—
A few how-dare-you's but that's about it
waking from a sleepwalk

Now the happy guy he used to be's a
soldier in the east and
when it snows a mountain rises
and when she dials the telephone rings
in another world

A FUNNY CATARACT OF PATTERN

has infected time's eye
for future gazing
A rollicking flux of lines
running fire in between. You feel it in
stages down through heart to gut
and happy round the hips

See who's coming on
blowing through the gathered mist
a lilting pipe
How much does he need of
care and pruning, water, tears

What's left to weakness slotted
How far can he cast a net
for audience or contact
or reach to grab a staff by which
to poke his way across the spreading stream

SOAR KESTREL, EYEING FUR

Motion lights on wire
A portion of intelligence
A creek-viewed bump of plump
something. Oars out
you've come this far
face blazing, glazed cranium
One part pearl, two-knit bone and one
of fire. The dream-on

You can't unravel yet you
quarrel with her when she won't
work in portions clear and bright
The red truck years ago, a roadside picnic
mountain park. Time bound
          in fear knots
loosened. Then you had a right to play
          as poles passed
What kind of look next looks like places
people I have known
Shadows from her face did fall

SUMMER 2014, MISSING ANSELM

for Anselm Hollo

To write is what, a concertina
squeezing in and out, a mission
holding passages attuned
to wilderness, stunning in their
suddenness. Mind, trying to catch up
surrenders. All the dancing
happens in the dawn, in terms unknown
til they arrive already mixed
with light of nowhere come from

Washing windows
Picking up a fallen trunk to lay across a stream
Wobble as you go, and then a narrow path
brings you to a tavern—
Event and image rise
and when you least expect it
Pay dirt—that's the beauty
and the horse it rides on
breathing—guests of space
A vision from the hill, another day

YEAH YOU SAID THAT DID YOU MEAN IT

And what do I mean in coordination with
other kinds of feeling in relation to
events. Sit and listen to
oneself played back—
Continual compromise of this
suit by that piece of armor
Too much instant know-how to pre-figure
knowing much. Can't help dabble
dib-dab here and paddle there
Webs nipped by snapping turtles
How this way opinion flies
absorbs deflection and comes to a conclusion
for the good of all
which sets the next imbroglio up

O for a borrowed dream exit-lined in cornrows
and briars woven from a crumpled bed
Hallelujah the king of mind's
restored, driven by a waste dump
a cello starts
occulting light. A mattress flies
and tendency to peter out receives new
inspiration—All's possible now
A new design, an old world
to be used again for parts

SOON BUT THE END IS LONG

Late park notice
short-stitched, one part
sun, part
cast-off, cloud-draped
Wind
slaps against a raft
Barrels
rolled up flipped
on gravel
Fish, extended
frame dissolves
Big pause you say
"Hippo"
glistens
Waterhole
necks drink
through throats
Girl mouse on a
rock laps
fallen light's
delicate
decisions
Silence
fills the surface

FLAVORS OF A SINGLE TASTE

The world's active in its lives
this morning as the creek arrives
Only what one "wants to" disappears
never had the last word
Even so, ducks dabble

I'm learning to erode the Palisades
into the Hudson
Home is what you least remember
having forgotten
settled elsewhere

Sky spreads black with cloud
portraits—calligraphic instants
Time's journey held in baskets
roaming coastlines
Biscuits dipped in and out of tea

KEEP ON TIL YOU MAKE THE END-AROUND

Sky and branches, faded lilacs
wild lettuce, high weeds
Birds still have their hearing
Old pachyderm's low lip, v-formed
picks a bunch of violets

Adept at air and earth
she takes a drink and breathes in
what she has to carry
gives it up unspoken at the end
I've no idea

Light trunk transfer
grafted to a world that doesn't care
but makes accommodation for
pachyderm and rat
You raise a knee to slip the opposition

CAN'T STAY AS LONG AS I WANTED

Young bucks kept off as long as I could
ordered in their orderly confusion
A couple of cocks doodled on a wall
in serpentine rhythm
Where is the weather lady? Mr. Species
woke up cool beside the Mrs.
No one knew the shoes
they wore or
which one's laughter
poised upon that rock
surveying surf-swirl

Transposed memory gems
in basement start to move and talk
The system's singing, sighing with
mushrooms on a turf
Accidents weaving sentences to no apparent purpose
but the poem's

A JOYFUL STRAIN
A WINCE OF PAIN

for Mei-mei Berssenbrugge

There as
she plays
her
stringed instrument
whose sounding
box is my
mood

Spicatto
adagio e
presto, a smile
and sigh, a lift of
eye

Who
wasn't once
in partial place
looking back
to rain or shadow?

Curiously shed
of notes
dropped on a lotus
Gathering rays
to comb
her morning practice

IN AN INSTANT

Further thought arrives as plague
unwanted, not to be reconciled
The thrill is gone, well, that's the feeling
Mindfulness obstructed
             A snagged flute

The catch: no assurance
Birdsong hummed in through the yard
No scheme of things, reason for season or
cosmic sense to the order you're in

Too much one thought, too much that thought
No accomplishing vehicle
             stripped of its design
No guru as guide, purified mind-flame, just
             ideas inside a cabin

But there is something in the way she shifts
downturned eyes, a quizzical gleam
             finally, of what?
The whole gist happened
under surface, you may remember
             happily not knowing the way

POINT OF RECOGNITION

She is looking down a well
as deep a lover's profile as
the old-man-of-the-mountain's

Powerful in pride, the boundary porous
How dependent all this is
on light for making shadows

On a ledge that holds some
inner power, she is standing
clearly developing that
seen by others with such interest in
what sees and what it has been led to
say in writing

re the stars' apprehension—
Everyone can look in
deeply settled eyes

and step through walls, listening
as writing in the reading
holds her profile—nose and chin

with lips in anxious speculation
We have all we need to know
but there is something else that makes her really
    say it

IN THAT LOOK SHE GETS IT RIGHT

Tenderness worn close to the surface
A most forbidding dragon suit
The day promised extension

How to adjust—I don't want to simply mark it
"saved"—the drive. The word "truck" has
opened out—A crescent wrench

What she does fits and turns down tight until
a party of warm light begins
none of it classified as to type
fonts and sizes all stuffed in

Shining forth from underneath
a pageant collective's autumn
        drive
Everything else will have to wait

The wolf a few blocks down
delivers milk with Martha Raye-like eyes
Enough to make this particular
Joan of Arc glide conscientiously to her stake

WASHES HER HAIR

Pulled over the front of her face
in a fist and squeezed—
Thus every other day's oblation
rinses, offering dust
to the god of new beginnings

Why not, so tired, offer your best
residue? Stories are powerful
What do they mean as
providence or provenance? A message
combed in and out of eyes

When one needs an ancient Greek response
O chest, allow my tongue to lift, say
    what's on the horizon
Talking clouds, salt-fresh, ready
Exhaust pipe smoking on a bank of snow

INCREMENTS AND A FINALE

In its place propose
a crash test, unstable
flap-eared character with staff
in colloquy's
uncertain terms. Doppler
moves across the waves
Inertia's castaway
drifting off the Cornish coast
Intelligible
patterns, shoe beat
Roll your shimmering bottleneck
Constable
Incorporate details
ramped from houses
What's left of memory
cigarettes?
Intermittent collar scratch
Geez, I think
Raisins can't travel farther than
oysters. Who'll get home first?
Great idea for calendar
Pickle-of-the-Month

ONE SOMETHING MAKES ANOTHER

stall, convicts it of perplexity
A shelf of U.S. dish soaps
The name on a plate of hammered steel
there where moments of truth reside
between molecular face-offs

A currant of course is a berry
There is no name for the rise of scalp
    before beheading
The prospect of pain a testicular grip
Another bad idea exposed by lightning

Now, that is sitting with a corpse
right on the facet of a diamond
The last card dealt as you
slide your finger toward the
minefield—play it cold
or up in flames, or like a roll
of dough upon a stone
see it's you unfolding in the midst

GOOD CLEAR SEEING

in pockets
but overall a blur about what to do with
the intuitive part, tracing light
from a knocked-over lamp
Neurosis of need, blanket of grain
All that you know about being alone
The energy from up the perineum

What happens today is unknown
Everything re-arranged after the fall
How many parts are keyed to eyes
adding disparate pieces to the field?

        Nuts and shells
        Loss of stem
        Source rites, avocets in shoals

What does it mean to be a school?
Hard to argue apparent fate
    with demons in the shrubbery
Don't speak too soon about what's to come
It's walking on thin ice

WELL

Even from this hole looking out
there is enough of sky and treetops
to see how each of us is taught
the major objects of the world

The robin and Western Disposal
invite us to this land of doings, systems
no one can control or get away from
but lives at the edge of

Animated by premonitions
in a body waiting for times to come
When cold air hits the flue that draws it up
into an urn of bliss

Stay put
Habit drags one's feet and pulls one's hair
but fortunes marry
fire, air, going up together

WHAT CONSORT AND RANGE OF PLAY

The sun shines in its last great movement
Moon emerges looking on the scene
Sky's delivered from thought-anguished
       wrapping—Such losses can be shared and
       turned to joy

Is every movement more or less
       expansion? Mutual support is given
       differently
       at this depth

The guru's hand imbued with such intention
Without question you deserve this range of play

Trying to be warm, the letting-go is
       magnetism that the board turns on
A switch becomes
       a closet. Open!
Music changes
Fleeting instants belt
       transfer pulses
What's the rhythm necessary now?

Tongues smart from the current groove selected
Conduct through roots to upturned
       leaves the deepest sum of heaven's
       overtones

ENTRANCE BASED IN FEELING

In an uncompromised room
of dedicated passivity, you do this for me and I will
pay you back. But the reciprocity is not quite here
Leaves fall from OK, fine, but
I have not yet surrendered enough individual rights
in the name of brotherhood

What's coming in is bottled time. We pour
a drink, it burns. In the blink of an eye
the kingfisher flies. What was I supposed to gather
for how long? Purposefully balanced
see-saw partners
How much do we really want to know about
getting things together?
And through what ray or tonic?

There is the feeling "pour"
"pouring" and "while." Go live
along that way, and in between
avoid—unsew—what you saw coming
at the time through portholes bouncing. Escape
by undiscovered caverns. Look both ways before
distraction, definitely wanting flavor of the saints
floods your journal

MELANCHOLY LINES THE BASKET

Grapes and leaves insulate from drafts
in lower places, establishing a mood
repository. A beaded curtain swings
inviting one to check out hibernation holes
Gulls overseeing distribution

Though your cookbook may have lost a
signature or two, it was the one you salvaged
at the time. You passed it on
to whom? To lower places
in the mood repository

Reward of days
wherein you may remember something as a prayer
Words of little use
but always joy in feeling them
Come say it

What appears will never take you down
Belief in simple promise
and exchange. Halfway to the door
an exit to a lower elevation
A serpent passing into vines

LIKE A RUGGED MOUNTAIN OF GLASS

From ledges and sheer drops
the body tilts and wavers
into form
Sounds echo, sights
vibrate in color with flames
baring their shoulders

There's only so much meaning we can make
and then return to
spine and crown
charged from underneath
invigorating what remains
Attention like a mountain of glass

Please come and be a sun of wisdom
branching in and going out in
fiber-optic radiance
crumbling into piles of sand
blown here and there around the city's end

AND THAT'S THE GOOD NEWS

Insertions of perfect timing in
a latitude of being—
   Sing a song in bolts and snatches
Good to manufacture enthusiasm
   for resonance but
   who will ever buy
the tune the finches tell
   with doves behind as chorus

Anselm in the great objectivist tradition—
   object as the subject
   of the object in the subject

Let it settle, melt, and co-descend
   Now it re-arises
where you live, down low, comes into a breath
that lets you un-think for a blessed minute
Listen. She's not there, the woodpecker
calculating by her long, hard nose
   patterns necessary to expose the day
   without losing her mind

IN THREADS OF THIS WEB

run peeps from a seaside years ago
like a kitchen's stainless counter
with pans, whisks, ladles
suspended above
the coming day

You see them
orchestrated from behind
Ruddy turnstones
Oystercatchers
holding to a spit of land
Water sparkling for attention

The puffer says it too
with feeling—
What's taking so long
introducing sunlight
to this hazy web?
An engine fish swim in and out of

SOMEBODY'S CRACKING THE WHIP

The Wakemans call early
to cancel arrangements made earlier
Year of the tiger—lots of upheaval
squawking—You can't close the window
A risky defile

Who needs these pricks
of dysplasia to get to the bottom
and climb back up? Thunder and Whimsy
pull at their reins—
Stammer steps mass an intrusion

Let me stay where I am—I've brought it on myself
Cast of thousands—
Let me distinguish the difference
among pools of time
drained back into immanence

Taken from countless preludes
More dollars than days
When sensibility doesn't fit temper
give it no response—let them swirl
I'm alone in this dale

Death and quitting time make loopholes
in everyone's contract. Don't make it worse
My mother can't darn them now
You can't escape the rose on its thorns
though many have tried on the glove

RAPTURE PLOUGH

Living impulse in a vault of flowers
An arc of networked
oratory. Raven sable
on a platform calls for
garment-choice as discipline

There it is, warmth rising
Fan-ripples on a windless pool
articulating laps of light in
mortifying stages—
Ways it could have been otherwise

Define clarity, absolute
hope's despair-coined
image. A classic tenor fades
into the hedge. Never do anything
but provide a ladder over

What world has been given this leg up?
Afraid of what might have been let down
resurrection finds a road
no field left unturned
Exactly which one is the hedge you live in?

I KNOW WE SAY THIS BUT

how many removes from us is it?
How many lovers of Wordsworth
find meditation
when everything else has fallen
into the pond
ears tuned to particular tonalities

What could be simpler
The oblique blade
leaves us wanting to be home
A crooked insect
emerges stumbling
from vast and waffled being
One reason to always begin as a child

FROM THE BROW OF THIS RIDGE

for Nathaniel Dorsky

Looking east a dust trail rises
Eagle shrieks, the breeze
becomes a set of sails
under which many hands are feeling

But since that picture hasn't been developed
Why go on when
things are moving, 7:10, etc.
No hat or gloves

Naked weight without volume
No scale to say how much of it is
still propped in the backseat
radiating

Making calls to worthy ones
Strength of mind all these years
drips off face and chest hair

Airplanes roar and rumble
overhead—the passenger within
sees the world's lucid and no one
can do anything about it

DAY WEARS ON AND MIND GROWS WIDE

Full of stuff—more and more
that won't get done
Crack goes the branch
You enter ligaments
that turn whichever way you think

Too many motions possible
recede in waves. Structure
suggests a job is good for focus
Otherwise the screw just turns
and turns, you need a grip
for slender passage to the sea

No port in sight—no bead to pare attention
for your progress. You've slipped
the need, cut adrift
and entered in a plane
with all kinds of tentacles
wriggling underneath. They coax you on
but Jim the cat and Slim the politician—
things lovely in their ways of drawing forth
must now be left to float

Show good amounts of flesh
What seems to be necessity
is looked on only dimly by the judge
who sees right through the center of this room
and asks the questions I live to avoid

WHEN WILL WE KNIT SOME
DRAGON UNDERWEAR

against this tenderness
breathing? When perspective's gained
and leaves a ring for flight
the promontory erodes
What listens to its bass-producing sounds?
At what point are they said to be in tune?

Something makes something else
beautiful and charged, knock-kneed
molecules dancing to the Dead

Only for an instant giving succor
When someone else says "brilliant"
there really is no use trying to re-capture
but clarify the window's view
A horse in willows mixing breath
and dew

You can't cover every base on
every play, but what's that scope that's rising
from below? A ball of wax
melts in light of a month's
wick licked by arrows and a crown

WHAT PLACE—IN WHAT PLACE

Ordinary cuckoo material
pleased in its plasticity—making a mark
A firsthand swoop
Even if unnoticed
there's clairvoyance
in obliquity, forced encounters
with mistrust, enjoyment without reservation

What is left for markets
not to have a stake in?
Although beauty comes and goes
the stars are still out-turned this
monster year for cocoanuts and transition

What is left to come through?
Ideopathies, of course. Let them come with
motivation, pride—Only you know
through what links
transmission flows. Sometimes you're on top
and twirling, sometimes books just
fold up in your hands

WORK PRECEDES THE MIRACLE

Establishing centers of repose and
favor, miraculous because they
disappear, unbenownst to
anyone, there isn't much to want
out here—a log-jam of benevolence
Some folks see the future as a chance
not-so-bright. I see it more
deepening to a point, and then
slipping off to one side
when the plate of least resistance gets too hard

To not go there might be a miracle
in someone else's life; in mine it's one
I'm into. Shame is
not to meet and have a drink with—who?
underground. It isn't a surprise this breaks
What kind of work preceded it?

Burrowing down until things open
Even then the rocks are hard for seeing
Think of everyone who's lived and died
There have been some really weird ones
and you are not always free and happy—
It's a question of translucency

LIKE THE LAST DAY OF SUMMER

This winter day's uncomprehended
circumstances smiled and
popped in unannounced. How is our side
supposed to hold—How does your heart do it?
A glass of whiskey is the kind of potent friend
I think you need. For the moment you are not alone

But you wake up again, a kind of waking
anyway. Of many kinds
which one is this? The one you're in
Never mind, bright or dim
or warm is what you get, a drawing
in and out. It would be good to let it fall
as the horizon waves and crashes
driving home. Your real friends have seen you
naked, hopeless. They have led the way

There is nothing about what you need in this
or what you want to say. It's just
a coating burned off in the stratosphere
Nothing to break laws about
Even if you could you wouldn't
rise into the clouds and disappear

NOT MUCH OF A HOLD PERHAPS

Rope slack in the sun
A breathing thing
simply feels
rills and spills, electro-magnetic
core-induced spiral-—no origin

A humming reed's empty
glow, waving back and forth
underwater. Span and glide
up to ears
running down one's neck and shoulders

Light, the water's simple
energy and bliss at last comes
clear. We ride it as it flows
unincorporated
Hard to find a fence against which

accelerations may be measured
Having developed teeth
we eat but what to
leave behind—earth becoming water
drying in the sun

HERE'S SOMETHING TO DO

Green air, black ant
adapts to a place unlooked for
She wants a lace top
That's erotic on my part
Things want to be alive
Are you sure?
Yes, there is nothing else to want
Get high, what else is known
about what's guaranteed?
What does the sun want to climb on?
Read this book
A Midsummer Night's Dream. Find out
where you go when you don't
know. Let someone else's sleep
carry you on its back
into the forest
into a fairy ring
There are many places
to not quite fully enter. Fully enter one
What do you mean? Come for a dance
(That's what I mean) and we will
try to follow

BECAUSE BURNS HAS BEEN SUNG
AND SHAKESPEARE TOO

What is left for me to try to do?
Methinks I see things with a partial eye
Everything looks double—Hermia wakes
What has seemed more than one thing all these
    nights
comes sliding out across the floor

Puck, invisible operator
jangles perspectives, motives
What's exposed—your ass's head
confused in service. Present chaos bodes
future harmony. Needs in disarray

Don't give up, surrender. Roll down
to the spring-house, mossy place
where one dream then another drips
from pipes in revelation
All you have to do
is enter through the bloodstream

We've been asking different questions
of time transformed. They drop
into the spring-pool
of this—might as well admit it—
arbitrary life

BITTERSWEET

Where did you want to go today?
   Completely free, available to all
The sunlight on the stones
   Your eye, your mind
Which would you prefer to give
   as artist, scientist, psychologist, meditator
or simply as voyeur

This is the person in his or her world
   I must be me in mine
In sunlight or in shade, I follow
   each facet in its set
each grain its flavor, county, weather
   Salt-sand on a rocky shore
Palming a hand across my present brow

To see it wholesome stop pretending
   it doesn't slow or speed up
Who cares whether
   at a certain point
we have to abandon the search
   "What is it coming to anyway?"
A scent of former darkness

THE LAST IMPUTED VOICE CAME
FROM A CABIN

A wrinkle in your latest playlist charted
Source of what's name—interior stuff
Another course another song imported
Close-quarters, infinite? No chance
for perfect policy but chaste
moving from the woods a vision of
great kindness. That much felt
without question, seems so. When two-headed
pigeons flew over no one blinked
even when we left the ground to see them

No one is a witness dying
capturing rays from apparent particles
and letting them back out—
The window compared to a ship

If morning were a long boat
traveling along a long coast, scouting harbors
sisters, brothers re-unite and children
enter into one another. As it is
listen to these strings of fate-plucked harmony
Songs of love for all and not for long

THIS DAY FELL FROM

for Linda Morgan

One morning all that was was
all together. No more spoken
on the little typewriter
The room looked the way it did
The road above the bank was

there, if not actively uncovered
Seeds sprouted new participants
A trace remained, having been introduced
to others at ground level
Many did this, welcomed in the past

To erase it would be messy and complex
To start anew, one can't be blind
to all that's entered in and still pulls strings
at joints with tensions of
response, wondering forever who we are

Outside, leaves and needles fall
conditioning the soil, funny kinds of fungus
pop through to sun and rain
All this seems to end but keeps on
taking form, each another's variation

THUS WE ARE REAL

this real—
everyone agreeing or
disagreeing. Reality a day
or long night. Many
came together and then "What's left?"
The question was
how to get home when the love
in your heart is still where it
was trying to get out of
What use to know what's never known?
Old shows of hurt
It doesn't matter
How was he with the babes?
See how she runs
past the mark
A new ear grown
beneath her own, "Come and give"
she says
but for which generation?
A story moving on horizon scale

Photo by Laurie Adato

Reed Bye lives in Boulder, Colorado with his wife, Jill Jones. He has published ten collections of poetry and two albums of original songs. He recently retired after many years on the core faculty of the Jack Kerouac School at Naropa University, where he taught poetry writing workshops and courses in classic and contemporary literary studies, and contemplative poetics.

60641585R00043

Made in the USA
Charleston, SC
03 September 2016